Essentials of
Goal Setting

Shyam Bhatawdekar

Dr Kalpana Bhatawdekar

Essentials of Goal Setting

Books by Shyam Bhatawdekar and Dr Kalpana Bhatawdekar

1. *HSoftware* (Human Software) (The *Only* Key to Higher Effectiveness)
2. Sensitive Stories of Corporate World (Management Case Studies)
3. Classic Management Games, Exercises, Energizers and Icebreakers (Volume 1)
4. Classic Management Games, Exercises, Energizers and Icebreakers (Volume 2)
5. Stress? No Way!! (Handbook on Stress Management)
6. *HSoftware* (Shyam Bhatawdekar's Effectiveness Model)
7. Competencies and Competency Matrix
8. Soft Skills You Can't Do Without (Goal Setting, Time Management, Assertiveness and Anger Management)
9. Essentials of Work Study (Method Study and Work Measurement)
10. Essentials of Time Management (Taking Control of Your Life)
11. Essentials of 5S Housekeeping
12. Essentials of Quality Circles
13. Essentials of Goal Setting
14. Essentials of Anger Management
15. Essentials of Assertive Behavior
16. Essentials of Performance Management & Performance Appraisal
17. Health Essentials (Health Is Wealth)
18. The Romance of Intimacy (How to Enhance Intimacy in a Relationship?)
19. Good People: *Novel, a refreshingly different love story*
20. Funny (and Not So Funny) Short Stories
21. Stories Children Will Love (Volume 1: Bhanu-Shanu-Kaju-Biju and Dholu Ram Gadbad Singh)
22. Travelogue: Scandinavia, Russia

To Our Family

Shyam Bhatawdekar   Dr Kalpana Bhatawdekar

For assured growth and progress of desirable dimensions in personal, professional, family and social life every person should resort to "Goal Setting" on a perennial basis. It should become a natural habit with every ambitious person who is out to find meaning in life.

"Goal Setting" if done properly helps you to define your dreams and aspirations in more clear and concrete terms in the form of achievable goals. Then it becomes easy to take the required actions to achieve the desired end results.

Considering its huge benefits in all walks of human life a thorough knowledge of "Goal Setting" becomes imperative. To facilitate gaining the knowledge in this vital subject in the shortest time, authors Shyam Bhatawdekar and Dr Kalpana Bhatawdekar included only the "essentials" of "Goal Setting" in the book.

The authors are top-notch business executives, successful entrepreneurs, highly sought after business and management consultants, eminent management gurus and scholars, authentic human behavior experts and prolific authors. And so the book becomes an authentic document on the subject.

To read more by the authors, refer their websites: http://shyam.bhatawdekar.com, *http://writings-of-shyam.blogspot.com* and http://management-universe.blogspot.com

5

Essentials of

Goal Setting

Shyam Bhatawdekar
Dr Kalpana Bhatawdekar

Published by Publishing Division of

Prodcons Group

8, Pranjal Society, Shiv Tirth Nagar, Paud Road, Pune
411038 (India)

Email: prodcons@prodcons.com

For other web publications, refer: http://management-
universe.blogspot.com and
http://shyam.bhatawdekar.com

Contents

Essentials of Goal Setting

What is Goal?

The dictionary meaning of goal is: aim, purpose, target, objective, achievement or end result.

Goal is a desired result one contemplates or envisions and then commits or promises to achieve. One has then to plan for it, muster the necessary efforts and resources and direct them towards achieving the goal within a predefined time frame.

That's why just imagining about a goal is not equal to setting a goal. That can be called only daydreaming. But with goal setting or target setting you are in fact getting ready to get in action to take steps to actually achieve the goal. That way you are acting to convert your dreams into reality. You have to make things happen to achieve a goal.

What's Goal Setting?

Goal setting is also called "target setting". Setting up or deciding upon the goals or outcomes in more definable terms that you wish to achieve at the end of a specific period is termed as goal setting.

Therefore, the goals you set or decide will be expressed as: more tangible than intangible, more quantitative than qualitative, more objective than subjective, more specific than vague, more measurable than non-measurable, more time bound than without deadlines etc.

The goal setting is done for setting out your various goals from time to time on matters related to many spheres of your life as per the context.

Edwin A Locke developed goal-setting theory in 1960s. His first article on goal setting theory was "Toward a theory of task motivation and incentives". He published it in 1968. This article triggered the ongoing thought process on goal setting. It indicated that a positive relationship exists between clearly identified/defined goals and performance.

Context

Goal setting or target setting can be done in:

- Personal,
- Family
- Organizational and
- Social context

Goal/Target Setting Duration Span

Goal or target setting is done on:

- Short term (from few weeks to one year),
- Medium term (one to three years or so) and
- Long term basis (three years to ten years or so)

In the context of personal goals, one can even think of setting up lifetime goals. Lifetime goals mean what you want to achieve over your entire life, how you will like to shape up your life, how you will like to be remembered by the people.

Purpose of Goals

- To channelize your ideas
- To establish priorities
- To focus your attention

- To give right direction to your efforts
- To facilitate drawing the road map based on the set goal
- To give you a time frame to work and in which to plan
- To keep you away from wasting your efforts/resources
- To keep you away from non-value adding activities
- To keep on track (quality, direction and time wise)
- To help motivate yourself and others
- To ensure everybody is clear about what is happening
- To improve the overall performance levels
- To help reward yourself when the task is complete
- To build self-confidence

Goal Setting: Perennial Exercise

Goal setting is not a one-time job. It is a recurring job. Day after day, month after month and year after year you will have to achieve some goal or the other in personal, professional, family and social spheres of your life in order to lead you life successfully and meaningfully.

Several of your goals may run concurrently in a given period and so also your goal related activities.

With the passage of time your priorities of goals may

undergo changes. For example at times your career-oriented goals may take priority, at other times the family related goals may become the most important and there will be times when health related goals might move on to the top spot.

Goal Setting Positively Impacts Performance

One can always keep working endlessly even without setting the goals; it is not necessary that one is obliged to define the goals.

However, it is observed that the people who identify and define their goals in more specific and clear terms outperform the people who do not do so. Their effectiveness and efficiency improve as a result of their goal setting exercise.

By undertaking the goal setting exercise the expected end results or outcomes become more understandable in terms of:

- Their size/quantum, quality and time frame
- The roadmap and the milestones to achieve them

become more visible.

- Clarity emerges on resources and techniques/technology requirement.

Overall impact of it is to improve effectiveness and efficiency and thus the overall performance levels of individuals and teams.

Goals Are Motivators

When people set goals and achieve them, it gives them tremendous satisfaction. They feel like performers and winners. The goal becomes the standard of measurement of their effectiveness, efficiency and success. And when they achieve that standard it gratifies them. Their self-esteem or self-respect increases. Then they feel motivated to take on the subsequent goals.

They get motivated to the extent that they can undertake still higher and bigger goals subsequently. We call them stretch goals. Thus goal-setting exercises are self-fulfilling and provide the necessary encouragement to undertake larger or higher level tasks and objectives.

Process of Goal Setting

When setting goals you should follow this sequence:

1. **See it:** Visualize your personal, professional, family and social aspirations. What are your dreams for each one these domains of your life? Dreaming is not bad provided you are also thinking in terms of giving your dreams some concrete shape. When you start thinking of converting your dreams into reality, you start visualizing them in more details. That's where your goal setting exercise starts. You start seeing the physical shapes/pictures and numbers and time lines. When how much of your dream will be turned into its physical shape and how? You are now setting goals mentally.

2. **Say it:** Holding your aspirations and goals only in your mind does not help. You must verbalize them. Start talking about it to yourself and/or with the relevant persons. It gives clarity to your thoughts. It provides a sounding board. Try to elicit the response and feedback. You are likely to improve upon your ideas and goals.

Few rounds of reflecting on them take you to the next step i.e. writing them down.

3. **Write it down:** Now take out paper and pencil and jot down your ideas (the dream, the vision, the mission) and related details of converting them into concrete objectives (what you propose to do to fulfill your dream, what actions are required to achieve what kind of quantifiable results by when?). Writing down is very essential part of the goal setting process. It facilitates to fill in the gaps found in your thinking and speaking, it brings in specificity, removes conflicts in various related issues and then it becomes a permanent reference material and a basis for review.

4. **Do it:** What you did so far in the first three steps is only the planning part of the entire process. Unless you start executing your action plan, you haven't even taken the first step in real sense to meet your aspirations. You have to take actions for implementing your plan. The following equations seem to be true:

Great plan + Zero implementation = No effectiveness, No results, No success

Some plan + Some implementation = Some effectiveness, Some results, Some success

Great plan + Great implementation = Great effectiveness, Great results, Great success

You can see here that the implementation or execution is the key factor for being effective and successful.

Goals Should Be SMART

Goals you set should be:

1. **Specific (S):** Your goal should not be vague, casual or general. It should be specific. Here are a few examples of what it means. Instead of setting a goal that I wish to reduce my weight, you should say I want to reduce my weight by 10 kilograms. Instead of setting a goal that says owning a three-bedroom house is my goal, you must paraphrase it to say owning a three-bedroom house in a decent locality in Irvine is my goal. Instead of stating that I want to improve my formal educational qualifications, you must clearly specify the course you wish to complete like MBA (Marketing) or MS

17

(Computer Science) or some other from a particular university. In fact your goal statement should be able to answer the questions like what, how much, why, who, where, how, when etc.

2. **Measurable (M):** You must give concrete measurable dimensions to your goal. If you are not in a position to measure your goal it becomes a very vague affair. In order to measure your goal or state it in quantifiable and verifiable terms you must also select a suitable criterion or unit of measurement. In an earlier example you can specify the area of your three-bedroom house in square feet. You can specify that I wish to own a house admeasuring 3500 square feet. Instead of saying that you will pass your MBA course with flying colors you must aim at achieving a specific percentage of marks or GPA score or rank in the university.

3. **Agreed (A)/Achievable or Attainable (A):** You must make sure that you can achieve the goal. For example a person who has been very weak in math and science over the years will find taking up the engineering degree courses non-achievable. In earlier example of weight reduction if you set a goal of losing all the 10

kilograms weight in two weeks it is not attainable. Perhaps what is attainable is losing one kilogram a week or every two weeks. The goal that is achievable should also have your full commitment or agreement. Make sure that you really are committed to achieve the chosen goal and do not have a lackadaisical or lukewarm attitude. It will be a good idea to promise not only to yourself but to some other relevant person (say your spouse in case of a personal or family goal or to your boss or colleague in case of a professional goal) that you have chosen a particular goal and you promise to fulfill it. It puts a positive moral pressure on you.

4. **Realistic/Relevant (R):** You should set realistic goals. For example going on a world tour at an early age in life is quite a far-fetched goal for a person with moderate earnings. Increasing the income ten folds in a single year also seems somewhat unrealistic goal for most people. Also the goal should be relevant- it should not be outright non-value adding or it should not be totally irrelevant to your top-level life goals. For example if your important life goal is to maintain good health throughout your life, your some other goal should not be to win a competition of eating

19

hamburgers or having a great night life once every week.

5. **Timed/Timely/Time-bound/Time Sensitive (T):** You must set a time frame to achieve your chosen goal. Without specifying the time by which you plan to achieve your goal, your goal remains only a hollow dream or wishful thinking. Fixing up the deadlines brings in urgency and importance. You become more sincere and serious. You mean business then. Also knowing over what period you need to achieve a goal helps you to track down and measure your progress of moving towards the goal at any point in time. In earlier example where you set the goal of reducing your weight by 10 kilograms, you must specify the date by which you will achieve it.

Now you can write your SMART goals easily.

The acronym "SMART" first appeared in November 1981 issue of 'Management Review'. It was referred to by its creator George T Doran in his article, "There's a S.M.A.R.T. way to write management goals and objectives".

Parkinson's Law

It is important that you set your objectives clearly, plan systematically and execute in a pre-decided time frame. Otherwise, the famous Parkinson's Law starts working for you. It says, "work expands to fill the time available for it's completion". Therefore, one should work "smarter" and not only "harder".

Domains of Organizational Goals: Examples

- Growth targets
- Revenue/profit improvement targets
- Sales targets
- Enhancement of customer base targets
- New product development/introduction targets
- Customer relationship/service improvement targets
- Quality improvement targets
- Cost reduction targets
- Lead time/cycle time reduction targets

Domains of Personal Goals: Examples

- Educational goals

21

- Competence building goals
- Personal grooming goals
- Assertiveness and confidence building goals
- Professional achievement/career goals
- Marriage related goals
- Children related goals
- Family related goals
- Financial and materialistic achievement goals
- Health related goals
- Entertainment/relaxation related goals

Difference between Goal Setting and Wishful Thinking

Most of the people do not go beyond "wishful thinking". And they mistake and confuse their wishful thinking with goal setting or target setting. More often than not, these people do not attain their wishes. Just desiring something or wishing something in a vague manner does not lead them to their achievements. It is difficult- if wishes were horses, everyone would ride. But in real life it is not seen that way.

There is a significant difference between wishes and putting wishes into a format of goal setting.

In large numbers of our seminars and workshops, when we request the participants to jot down their goals or targets, they scribble something like:

- Getting quicker promotions and raise in salary
- Getting rich
- Owning a nice house
- Traveling to foreign countries
- Blissful family life
- Excellent education to children

And so on.

Are these expressions of their targets or goals?

The answer is: These are definitely not targets or goals. They are mere wishes or desires. Goals or targets are much more than simply stating your desire or wish of wanting something to happen. For achieving your goal you need to clearly define exactly what you wish to accomplish otherwise your chances of success get significantly lowered.

Then how to convert these wishes into meaningful targets

or goals? We will show you by taking just one example.

Example:

The wish or desire is: Traveling to foreign countries.

Let us now create a goal or target out of this wish or desire.

Ask yourself following questions and answer them:

- Where do you wish to go first?
- When do you wish to go to the chosen foreign country?
- Will you be able to complete all the preparatory work before that date?
- Which cities in that country you want to visit?
- How long you intend staying there?
- Where do you plan to stay there: with your relatives/with your friends?
- How much money will be needed for to and fro airfare and other expenses during travel? Which route and airlines will you choose?
- How much money will be needed to stay there?
- How much money will be needed to travel various cities you wish to see in the foreign country?

- How will you take care of your medical expenses if any?

- Do you have this kind of money? What are your sources of money?

- Do you have a passport? If no, how much time it will take to get a new passport? Have you got all necessary documents?

- Do you have the required Visa to go to the foreign country? Do you have all the documents to get the Visa?

- Will you make your travel plans yourself or will you outsource it to an agency? What extra money you will need to hire the agency?

This may not be an exhaustive or comprehensive list. But you get a line of thinking and acting from this indicative list of questions.

You need to answer each one of them very specifically with facts and figures as correctly as possible. Then you will need to plan out the actions to be taken in order to complete the necessary tasks. The plan will have to be drawn on a time line.

Then you will have to get down to doing all those actions as per the timetable or schedule. And soon you will see that you are progressing towards achieving your goal day after day. And a day will arrive when you will have your passport and Visa with you, you will possess the required money (foreign currency) and you will be proceeding towards the airport to board your flight. Hey! You have achieved part of your above-mentioned goal. You will achieve rest of it after reaching the foreign country.

What did you really do? You really converted your wish or desire into a concrete goal or target by defining it as per the SMART criteria described in an earlier paragraph. In defining your goal in this new manner, you were SMART-your goal was now specific (S), measurable (M), agreed/achievable (A), realistic (R) and timed (T).

Specimen Goal Statements Qualifying SMART Criteria

Given below are a few goal setting statements that are near perfect that they meet the earlier mentioned SMART criteria. You may use them as model statements and work out your goal setting statements based on them.

1. My goal is to enroll in one of the top ten ranked business schools in USA to get a PhD in an important behavioral topic of human resource management by 20__ (specify the year).

2. My goal is to become manager of my existing department in the exiting company within next three years by honing my managerial skills consciously day after day and achieving all the business targets assigned to me and going beyond them by at least 20%.

3. My goal is to marry my girl friend (boy friend) by the end of the year in my girl friend's hometown in a day's religious ceremony keeping the ceremonial expenses below my one-month's salary.

4. Here onwards my goal is to go on a vacation with my spouse and children at least two weeks every year within my country or to any other country of my family's choice keeping the expenditure well within the bonus amount I get.

5. Our web site's goal is to increase the traffic to our web site by 100% by the end of the year resulting in 20%

increase in sale of our goods and services via our web site.

6. One of the goals of our customer service department is to respond to 100% of emails received from our customers or prospective customers within 24 hours of receipt of an email.

7. As the manager of my department my goal is to improve the motivational level of my team by increasing their participation through quality circles, task forces, team projects and linking rewards with performance resulting in the employee turn over rate below 2% and absenteeism below 5% annually.

8. As an author my goal is to write at least 10 pages every day thus finishing a 300 pages novel in a month, editing it the next month and publishing it by the end of every third month thus completing my target of writing and publishing 4 novels every year.

9. One of my this year's social networking rejuvenation goals is to send out the new year greetings by emails, greeting cards and phone calls to each and every

business, social and family associate so as to reach them before 31st December without missing anyone.

10. My goal is to dramatically reduce my endless conflicts with my spouse to bring them down to near zero within three months by learning the conflict resolution skills within next fortnight and then applying them with all the seriousness.

11. My goal is to reduce my weight to the ideal weight prescribed for my height and age by the fifth month from now by keeping a watch on my diet, exercises and life style as advised by my counselor.

12. As a management consultation organization our goal is to increase our clients by 25% by this year-end by approaching the prospective clients by way of direct mailers, presentations, free seminars, exhibitions and advertisements investing 10% of our previous year's profits on it.

13. I will like to learn French by taking a crash course of three months duration to start conversing in French proficiently though may not be able to write in it.

Some Interesting Quotes Related to Goals and Goal Setting

Given below are the quotes on goals and goal setting from some of the people thought to be successful in their own fields. It's worthwhile reading and understanding the important points they brought in about goals and goal setting. The subtle as well as specific points made in these quotes are worth noticing and these may become your additional learning points on this subject.

1. One's philosophy is not the best expressed in words; it is expressed in the choices one makes. In the long run, we shape our lives and we shape ourselves. The process never ends until we die. And, the choices we make are ultimately our own responsibility. - Eleanor Roosevelt

2. If you're bored with life- you don't get up every morning with a burning desire to do things- you don't have enough goals. - Lou Holtz

3. The important thing in life is to have a great aim and the determination to attain it. – Goethe

4. The real pleasure of one's life is the devotion to a great objective of one's consideration. - George Bernard Shaw

5. It doesn't matter where you are coming from. All that matters is where you are going. - Brian Tracy

6. Goals determine what you're going to be. - Julius Erving

7. Your goals are the road maps that guide you and show you what is possible for your life. - Les Brown

8. Living without an aim is like sailing without a compass. - Dumas

9. The future belongs to those who believe in the beauty of their dreams. - Eleanor Roosevelt

10. There are people who put their dreams in a little box and say, "Yes, I've got dreams, of course I've got dreams". Then they put the box away and bring it out once in a while to look in it, and yep, they're still there. - Erna Bombeck

11. Goals are dreams with deadlines. - Diana Scharf Hunt

12. Our goals can only be reached through a vehicle of a plan, in which we must fervently believe, and upon which we must vigorously act. There is no other route to success. - Stephen A Brennan

13. What's talked about is a dream, what's envisioned is exciting, what's planned become possible, what's scheduled is real. - Anthony Robbins

14. All our dreams can come true if we have the courage to pursue them. - Walt Disney

15. I have learned, that if one advances confidently in the direction of his dreams and endeavors to live the life he has imagined, he will meet with a success unexpected in common hours. - Henry Thoreau

16. Impossible is a word to be found only in the dictionary of fools. - Napoleon Bonaparte

17. The higher goal a person pursues, the quicker his ability develops and the more beneficial he will become to the

society. I believe for sure that this is also a truth. -
Maxim Gorky

18. Obstacles are those frightful things you see when you
    take your eyes off your goal. - Henry Ford

19. Fear melts when you take action towards a goal you
    really want. - Robert Allen

20. Nothing in the world can take the place of persistence.
    Talent will not; nothing is more common than
    unsuccessful men with talent. Genius will not;
    unrewarded genius is almost a proverb. Education will
    not; the world is full of educated derelicts. Persistence
    and determination are omnipotent. The slogan "press
    on" has solved and always will solve the problems of
    the human race. - Calvin Coolidge

21. Persistence is the ability to maintain actions regardless
    of your feelings. You press on even when you feel like
    quitting. When you work on any big goal your
    motivation will wax and wane like the waves hitting the
    shore. Sometimes you'll feel motivated, sometimes you

won't. But it's not your motivation that creates results - it's your action.

Persistence allows you to keep taking action even when you don't feel motivated to do so and therefore you keep accumulating results. Persistence will ultimately provide its own motivation. If you simply keep taking action, you'll eventually get results and results can be very motivating. - Zig Ziglar

www.ingramcontent.com/pod-product-compliance
Lightning Source LLC
Chambersburg PA
CBHW051418170526
45165CB00004BA/1868